SCHOLASTIC

Content-Building Learning Songs

by Meish Goldish

NEW YORK • TORONTO • LONDON • AUCKLAND • SYDNEY
MEXICO CITY • NEW DELHI • HONG KONG • BUENOS AIRES

Teaching *Resources*

For Chaya, the song in my life

Edited and produced by Immacula A. Rhodes

Cover design by Ka-Yeon Kim

Interior design by Sydney Wright

Interior illustrations by Maxie Chambliss, Sue Dennen, Kate Flanagan,
Rusty Fletcher, Anne Kennedy, Anthony Lewis, and Bari Weissman

ISBN-13: 978-0-439-60964-7

ISBN-10: 0-439-60964-X

Songs copyright © 2007 by Meish Goldish

Activities on pages 7–8 copyright © Scholastic Inc.

Published by Scholastic Inc.

1 2 3 4 5 6 7 8 9 10   40   14 13 12 11 10 09 08 07

Contents

Contents

Science

All About Animals

Habitats and Ecosystems

Plants

Earth and Sky

Health and Safety

Introduction

Welcome to *Content-Building Learning Songs*, a collection of irresistible songs that feature social studies, seasonal, and science topics children need to learn about in the early grades. The songs in this book are set to familiar kid-friendly tunes, making them easy to teach, fast to learn, and fun to sing!

You can use each song to introduce or reinforce concepts related to community helpers, neighborhoods, seasons, special days, animals, plants, and much more. The songs can be presented in a variety of ways. For example, you might copy them onto large chart paper, prepare transparencies for the overhead projector, or provide students with individual copies to use in class or at home. You can invite children to add their own illustrations to chart paper as a class project, or you can have them illustrate a specific section of a song on their own. Children might also choreograph their own hand or body movements to correspond to a particular song, and then perform their work for a small group or the entire class.

In addition to integrating the songs into your topical lessons, you can use them during circle time to provide sing-along shared reading experiences in which all children can feel successful. As with all read-aloud poems or rhyming songs, the songs in this book are a wonderful tool for teaching early literacy skills including print concepts, language patterns and rhymes, word recognition, and content area vocabulary. The songs can also be used to help ELL students learn and use new words in an appropriate context.

To get the most instructional benefit from *Content-Building Learning Songs*, we suggest that you become familiar with the songs and their tunes before using them with children. If possible, find the original song or tune on which each song is based—this can often be accomplished through a quick Internet search (some websites provide both the lyrics and audio versions of the songs). You might also play the original song for children so they can familiarize themselves with the tune. Then teach them the words of the selected song from this book and invite them to sing it together a few times. For longer songs, or for those with new vocabulary, you might divide the class into groups, assign each one a different verse of the song, and then have each group sing its verse aloud at the appropriate time. To spark creativity, invite children to play rhythm instruments while singing the song, make up movements to go along with the words, use related props during the performance, or add their own original verses.

Though there are many ways to approach and use the songs in this book, there's only one rule to follow: have fun!

Connections to the Standards

The songs and activities in this book are designed to support you in meeting the following standards outlined by Mid-continent Research for Education and Learning (McREL), an organization that collects and synthesizes national and state K–12 curriculum standards.

Language Arts
- Understands that print conveys meaning
- Uses mental images based on pictures and print to aid in comprehension of text
- Uses basic elements of phonetic analysis to decode unknown words
- Understands level-appropriate sight words and vocabulary
- Listens to gain information and for enjoyment
- Identifies rhymes and rhyming sounds

Geography
- Knows the location of a community and places within it
- Knows the physical and human characteristics of the local community
- Knows the similarities and differences in housing
- Understands that maps can represent surroundings
- Knows the modes of transportation used to move people, products, and ideas from place to place
- Knows how people affect the environment in negative and positive ways

History
- Understands personal family or cultural heritage through songs and celebrations
- Knows ways in which people share family beliefs and values
- Understand the reasons that Americans celebrate certain national holidays
- Knows the holidays and ceremonies of different societies

Science
- Knows how the environment changes over the seasons
- Knows vocabulary for different types of weather
- Knows vocabulary used to describe major features of the sky
- Knows that distinct environments support the life of different types of animals
- Knows that there are similarities and differences in the appearance and behavior of animals
- Knows that living things go through a process of growth and change
- Knows simple ways that living things can be grouped
- Knows that plants and animals have different features that help them live in different environments
- Knows that plants need certain resources for energy and growth
- Uses the senses to make observations about living things, nonliving objects, and events

Health
- Knows community health service providers and their roles
- Knows rules for traffic and pedestrian safety
- Classifies foods according to the food groups
- Knows basic personal hygiene habits required to maintain health

Kendall, J. S., & Marzano, R. J. (2004). *Content knowledge: A compendium of standards and benchmarks for K-12 education.* Aurora, CO: Mid-continent Research for Education and Learning. Online database: http://www.mcrel.org/standards-benchmarks/

Using the Songs to Extend Learning

Nearly all of the songs in *Content-Building Learning Songs* lend themselves to cross-curricular activities. The following activities include ways you can use the songs to extend students' learning:

Picture Book Songs

Children can turn the songs they learn into sing-along picture books. Invite them to copy each line of a song (or each verse) on a separate sheet of paper and illustrate it. Then have them arrange the pages in order, stack them between two sheets of construction paper, and staple the pages together to make a book. Tell children to write the song title on the cover, as well as the name of the tune the song is sung to.

Sing-Along Surprise

Build music into your day with a "sing-along surprise." Write each child's name on a slip of paper and place it in a bag or box. Explain that each day (or every Friday, for example) you'll select a child's name. This child will get to choose any moment of the day for the class to sing a song! Provide a bell—or some other method—for the child to signal that it's time for the sing-along. On the child's cue, stop what you're doing and enjoy a learning song together!

Name That Tune!

Invite groups of children to take turns humming a learning song from the book. Can the class name that tune? For example, if a group hums the tune of "Row, Row, Row Your Boat," students might guess "Traveling, Traveling," "Happy Halloween!" or "Walking Is Such Fun!" as the learning song that's sung to this tune. When children guess the song, encourage them to sing it aloud together. If they have identified more than one song for the tune, invite them to sing all of the songs!

Morning Meeting Songs

As you introduce new songs to children, copy them onto separate sheets of a chart paper pad. Each day, invite a different child to choose a song for the class to sing. Make a sparkly wand for children to use to point out the words as the class sings the song. For additional fun, let children decide whether they want to sing the song soft or loud, slow or fast.

Shake, Rattle, and Sing

Invite children to make simple instruments that they can use to create rhythms to songs they sing. Here are a few quick-and-easy instruments they might make:

* Have children cover a paper towel tube with paper and decorate it. Give them paper circles about an inch larger than the openings of their tube. Have them tape a circle over one end of the tube, place some dried beans or uncooked popcorn in the tube, tape a circle over the other end, and then shake! For more fun, invite children to tape streamers or curly ribbons to both ends of their shaker.

* Provide children with clean, lidded yogurt containers. Invite them to tap out rhythms with their fingers on the miniature makeshift drums. Or have them use the eraser-end of pencils as drumsticks.

* Create "washboards" for children to play. First, cut a large sheet of corrugated cardboard into 8- by 10-inch pieces. Then tape a strip of cardboard to the smooth side of each piece to make a handle. To play, have children slip their hand through the handle and scrape the corrugated side of the washboard with a craft stick, unsharpened pencil, or ruler.

* Give children plastic (or metal) spoons to tap together to play the "castanets."

Read-Along Recordings

Multiply the musical fun by letting children record the songs they learn on an audiotape. Place the tape and a cassette recorder in your listening center, along with copies of the songs. (For durability, you might laminate the songs and place them in a binder.) Then invite children to the center to listen to the songs and read along following the words on the song sheets.

Pocket Chart Word Play

Many of the songs in this book have lines that end in rhyming words. Write the words to these songs on sentence strips. Then cut apart the rhyming words. Place the sentence strips and word cards in a pocket chart. As you sing the song, invite children to replace the missing words. Encourage them to use the spelling patterns as clues. To extend the activity, invite children to suggest other words that rhyme. Write these words on sentence strips and trim to size. Then have children group the rhyming words and together look at the spellings. Do the same letters make the same sounds?

Living in the Country

(sung to "Sing a Song of Sixpence")

Living in the country,
Oh, what a treat!
Walking through a meadow,
Grassy and sweet.
Passing by a farmhouse
Where animals we see.
Certainly the country is
A special place to be!

Living in the country,
Oh, it is fun!
Sitting by a lake
To watch the setting sun.
Gazing up at night,
So many stars we see.
Certainly the country is
A special place to be!

City Life Is Swell!

(sung to "The Farmer in the Dell")

City life is swell,
City life is swell,
Tall apartments towering,
City life is swell!

Crowded stores and shops,
Crowded stores and shops,
Customers are everywhere,
City life is swell!

Museums, parks, and zoos,
Museums, parks, and zoos,
Many places we can see,
City life is swell!

Very busy streets,
Very busy streets,
Buses, cars, and taxicabs,
City life is swell!

The subway underground,
The subway underground,
Rumbling past and racing fast,
City life is swell!

City life is swell,
City life is swell,
Such excitement all around,
City life is swell!

When Firefighters Help!

(sung to "The Ants Go Marching One by One")

When firefighters start their day,
Hurrah, hurrah!
They're ready to help in every way,
Hurrah, hurrah!
They raise their ladders from the ground
And rescue people safe and sound.
Yes, we all give thanks
When firefighters help!

When firefighters get a call,
Hurrah, hurrah!
They bravely rush to help us all,
Hurrah, hurrah!
They spray their hoses all about
Until the fire has been put out.
Yes, we all give thanks
When firefighters help!

Oh, firefighters do such good,
Hurrah, hurrah!
They help protect our neighborhood,
Hurrah, hurrah!
Let's visit our fire station crew,
And thank them for the job they do.
Yes, we all give thanks
When firefighters help!

Police Help Keep Us Safe

(sung to "The Wheels on the Bus")

Police on the block are helping us,
Helping us, helping us.
Police on the block are helping us,
Helping keep us safe.

Police in patrol cars cruise the street,
Cruise the street, cruise the street.
Police in patrol cars cruise the street,
Helping keep us safe.

Police on horseback ride around,
Ride around, ride around.
Police on horseback ride around,
Helping keep us safe.

Police on scooters scoot on by,
Scoot on by, scoot on by.
Police on scooters scoot on by,
Helping keep us safe.

Police on foot walk up and down,
Up and down, up and down.
Police on foot walk up and down,
Helping keep us safe.

When You Go See a Doctor

(sung to "Miss Lucy Had a Baby")

When you go see a doctor,
When you go see a nurse,
They make you feel much better,
So you will not feel worse!

The doctor checks you over.
The nurse helps check you, too.
They both are very careful.
They know just what to do!

They check your ears and eyeballs.
They look right up your nose.
They do a check from head and neck
Down to your wiggly toes!

They listen to your heartbeat.
They take your weight and height.
They even look inside your throat
To make sure it's all right!

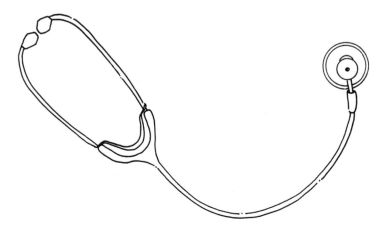

At work inside their office,
The doctor and the nurse
Are there to make you better,
So you do not feel worse!

In hospitals and clinics
Around the neighborhood,
The doctors and the nurses
Will help you to feel good!

Here We Go 'Round the Post Office

(sung to "Here We Go 'Round the Mulberry Bush")

Here we go 'round the post office,
The post office, the post office,
Here we go 'round the post office
To meet the postal workers.

These are the workers bagging mail,
Bagging mail, bagging mail.
These are the workers bagging mail
That comes out of the mailbox.

These are the workers stamping mail,
Stamping mail, stamping mail.
These are the workers stamping mail
To postmark every letter.

These are the workers sorting mail,
Sorting mail, sorting mail.
These are the workers sorting mail
By where each piece is going.

These are the truckers driving mail,
Driving mail, driving mail.
These are the truckers driving mail
To get it to the airport.

These are the pilots flying mail,
Flying mail, flying mail.
These are the pilots flying mail
To places far away.

These are more workers sorting mail,
Sorting mail, sorting mail.
These are more workers sorting mail
So it can be delivered.

These are the carriers bringing mail,
Bringing mail, bringing mail.
These are the carriers bringing mail
To put inside your mailbox!

We Love School!

(sung to "Three Blind Mice")

We love school, we love school!
School helps us learn, school helps us learn.
We learn to read all our words by sight.
We learn to add and subtract and write.
And learning in school is a real delight.
Oh, we love school!

We love school, we love school.
School is fun, school is fun.
We eat with classmates every day.
We like to go outside and play.
We laugh and joke along the way.
Oh, we love school!

We love school, we love school.
School is great, school is great.
Our class is nice, our class is fun,
Our class is great for everyone.
We stay all day 'til school is done.
Oh, we love school!
WE LOVE SCHOOL!

It's the Public Library

(sung to "Twinkle, Twinkle, Little Star")

There's a place that's fun for me.
It's the public library!
Lots of books for me to read,
Stories, poems, all I need.
There's a place that's fun for me.
It's the public library!

There's a place that's fun for me.
It's the public library!
Magazines for me to choose,
Newspapers with all the news.
There's a place that's fun for me.
It's the public library!

There's a place that's fun for me.
It's the public library!
Tapes and CDs I can play,
Videos to watch each day.
There's a place that's fun for me.
It's the public library!

Shop for Groceries

(sung to "Skip to My Lou")

CHORUS:
Shop, shop, shop for food.
Shop, shop, shop for food.
Shop, shop, shop for food.
Shop at the store for groceries!

Bread and muffins, good to eat,
Cereal made of oats and wheat,
Noodles, pizza, what a treat!
Shop at the store for groceries!

CHORUS

Apples, oranges, peaches, too,
Beans, potatoes, good for you,
Fruits and veggies, quite a few!
Shop at the store for groceries!

CHORUS

Beef and chicken, eggs and fish,
Turkey makes a tasty dish.
Burgers can be so delish.
Shop at the store for groceries!

CHORUS

Milk and yogurt, cottage cheese,
Buy some mozzarella, please.
Fill the cart with foods like these.
Shop at the store for groceries!

CHORUS

My Favorite Shops

(sung to "Do You Know the Muffin Man?")

CHORUS:

Do you know my favorite shops,

My favorite shops, my favorite shops?

Do you know my favorite shops

In the neighborhood?

The flower shop is really neat.

The flowers there smell, oh, so sweet!

Their pretty colors are a treat

In the neighborhood.

CHORUS

The toy store has so many things—

Yo-yos, cars, and kites with strings.

It even has a doll that sings

In the neighborhood.

CHORUS

The pet shop is the place I greet
All the pets I love to meet.
They bark, meow, and tweet-tweet-tweet
In the neighborhood.

CHORUS

The bookstore is where I relax,
Looking on the shelves and racks,
Hardcover books and paperbacks
In the neighborhood.

CHORUS

So Many Homes to See

(sung to "The Farmer in the Dell")

So many homes to see,
So many homes to see,
Different homes where people live,
So many homes to see.

A house, big or small,
A house, big or small,
It may be high, it may be low,
A house, big or small.

Apartments rising up,
Apartments rising up,
In buildings tall you see them all,
Apartments rising up.

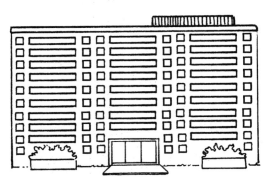

A farmhouse or a ranch,
A farmhouse or a ranch,
In the country you will find
A farmhouse or a ranch.

A mobile home on wheels,
A mobile home on wheels,
A home that rolls from place to place,
A mobile home on wheels.

A senior residence,
A senior residence,
Where seniors live together in
A senior residence.

A houseboat that will float,
A houseboat that will float,
On the water, you can see
A houseboat that will float.

So many homes to see,
So many homes to see,
Different homes where people live,
So many homes to see.

I Can Play There

(sung to "Found a Peanut")

There's a park here,
There's a park here,
There's a park here
In our town.
I can go there,
Play with friends there,
Watch the squirrels
And run around!

There's a playground,
There's a playground,
There's a playground
In our town.
I can seesaw,
Ride the swings there,
Dig in sand,
And run around!

There's a ball field,
There's a ball field,
There's a ball field
In our town.
I play kickball,
I play softball,
I play soccer,
And run around!

Just Use a Map!

(sung to "Did You Ever See a Lassie?")

CHORUS:
If you ever need directions,
Directions, directions,
If you ever need directions,
Then just use a map.

It's helpful for knowing
The way to be going.
If you ever need directions,
Then just use a map!

CHORUS

It's useful for learning
Which way to be turning.
If you ever need directions,
Then just use a map!

CHORUS

The east way or west way,
A map shows the best way!
If you ever need directions,
Then just use a map!

CHORUS

For neighborhood biking,
Or when you're out hiking,
If you ever need directions,
Then just use a map!

Hello, Neighbor!

(sung to "Goodnight, Ladies")

Hello, neighbor!
Hello, neighbor!
Hello, neighbor!
I'm glad that we are friends!

Merrily we get along,
Get along, get along.
Merrily we get along
In the neighborhood.

Smile big, neighbor!
Smile big, neighbor!
Smile big, neighbor,
To show that we are friends!

Merrily we joke around,
Joke around, joke around.
Merrily we joke around
In the neighborhood.

Call me, neighbor.
Call me, neighbor.
Call me, neighbor,
When you need a friend.

Merrily I'll help you out,
Help you out, help you out.
Merrily I'll help you out
In the neighborhood!

I've Been Watching the Construction

(sung to "I've Been Working on the Railroad")

I've been watching the construction
At the building site.
I've been watching the construction
As the building grows in height.
Listen to the hammers banging,
Jackhammers drilling in the ground.
Listen to the hammers clanging.
Such a noisy sound!

I've been watching the construction
At the building site.
I've been watching the construction
Going on from day to night.
See the workers as they're digging,
Digging up dirt and rock.
See the driver of the dump truck
Haul it off the block!

I've been watching the construction
At the building site.
I've been watching the construction
As each piece is placed just right.
Look at how the crane is lifting
Long steel beams into the air.
Look at how the beams are drifting
To the workers way up there!

I've been watching the construction
At the building site.
I've been watching the construction
And it's been a real delight!
Soon the work will all be finished,
And when the job is done for good,
We will have a brand-new building
In our neighborhood!

When Parades Come Through Our Town

(sung to "When the Saints Go Marching In")

Oh, when parades come through our town,
Oh, when parades come through our town,
Oh, how I love to watch and enjoy them,
When parades come through our town!

Oh, when the drums go boom, boom, boom!
Oh, when the drums go boom, boom, boom!
Oh, how I love to tap to the rhythm,
When the drums go boom, boom, boom!

Oh, when the horns go toot, toot, toot!
Oh, when the horns go toot, toot, toot!
Oh, how I love to sing with the music,
When the horns go toot, toot, toot!

Oh, when the cymbals start to crash,
Oh, when the cymbals start to crash,
Oh, how I love to snap my fingers,
When the cymbals start to crash!

Oh, when batons fly in the air,
Oh, when batons fly in the air,
Oh, how I love to watch all the twirling,
When batons fly in the air!

Oh, when the floats go rolling by,
Oh, when the floats go rolling by,
Oh, how I love to wave and cheer them,
When the floats go rolling by!

Oh, when parades march through our town,
Oh, when parades march through our town,
Oh, how I love to come out and join them,
When parades march through our town!

Read the Signs

(sung to "London Bridge Is Falling Down")

Read the signs that are around,
Are around, are around.
Read the signs that are around.
Signs can help you!

ENTER means to go in here,
Go in here, go in here.
ENTER means to go in here.
Signs can help you!

EXIT means to go out there,
Go out there, go out there.
EXIT means to go out there.
Signs can help you!

BIKE ROUTE tells you where to ride,
Where to ride, where to ride.
BIKE ROUTE tells you where to ride.
Signs can help you.

DO NOT ENTER means keep out,
Means keep out, means keep out.
DO NOT ENTER means keep out.
Signs can help you.

SLIPPERY FLOOR means watch your step,
Watch your step, watch your step.
SLIPPERY FLOOR means watch your step.
Signs can help you.

WET PAINT tells you not to touch,
Not to touch, not to touch.
WET PAINT tells you not to touch.
Signs can help you!

THIN ICE tells you don't walk here,
Don't walk here, don't walk here.
THIN ICE tells you don't walk here,
Signs can help you!

PHONE means you can make a call,
Make a call, make a call.
PHONE means you can make a call.
Signs can help you!

Traveling, Traveling

(sung to "Row, Row, Row Your Boat")

Ride, ride, ride a bike,
Pedal with your feet.
Traveling, traveling on a bike,
Biking is a treat!

Drive, drive, drive a car,
Drive it through the town.
Traveling, traveling on the road,
A car gets you around!

Take, take, take a bus,
Board and have a seat.
Traveling, traveling on a bus,
A bus just can't be beat!

Ride, ride, ride a train,
Ride along the track.
Traveling, traveling on the rails,
A train goes there and back!

Fly, fly, fly a plane,
High up in the air.
Traveling, traveling through the sky,
A plane will get you there!

Row, row, row a boat,
Gently round the lake.
Traveling, traveling on the water,
Boats are what you take!

Move, move, move your feet,
Move them on the ground.
Traveling, traveling on your feet,
Walk to get around!

The Bright Yellow School Bus

(sung to "The Itsy Bitsy Spider")

The bright yellow school bus
Is in the neighborhood,
Picking up the children
Everywhere it should.
It stops at each corner
To let the children on.
Then the bright yellow school bus
Very soon is gone.

The bright yellow school bus
Takes lots of kids to school.
Sitting on the bus,
They follow every rule.
They stay in their seats
And do not walk about
Until the yellow school bus
Stops to let them out.

The bright yellow school bus
Goes from block to block.
Kids on the bus
Keep their voices low to talk.
When school is over,
When the day has passed,
The bright yellow school bus
Takes them home at last!

The Very First Day of School

(sung to "Polly Wolly Doodle All the Day")

I'm happy when September's here,
It's the very first day of school!
Let's give a shout, let's give a cheer.
It's the very first day of school!

I'm set to start a brand-new grade,
It's the very first day of school!
With lots of new friends to be made,
It's the very first day of school!

CHORUS:
Hip hooray! Hip hooray!
The weather will soon be cool!
Vacation was fun, but now it's done.
It's the very first day of school!

Continued

I grab my backpack and ride the bus.
It's the very first day of school!
The teacher's waiting just for us.
It's the very first day of school!

In the classroom, we take our seats.
It's the very first day of school!
Our teacher hands out first-day treats.
It's the very first day of school!

CHORUS

I love how nice the classroom looks.
It's the very first day of school!
Our teacher passes out new books.
It's the very first day of school!

We read and write, we count and play.
It's the very first day of school!
Today is such a special day.
It's the very first day of school!

CHORUS

Happy Birthday!

(sung to "Alouette")

CHORUS:
Happy birthday,
Have a happy birthday.
Happy birthday,
A special day for you!

Will you sing a birthday song?
Yes, I'll sing a birthday song!
Birthday song,
Sing along!
Oh!

CHORUS

Will you blow your candles out?
Yes, I'll blow my candles out!
Candles out,
Clap and shout!
Birthday song,
Sing along!
Oh!

CHORUS

Will you share your birthday cake?
Yes, I'll share my birthday cake!
Birthday cake,
Here, please take!
Candles out,
Clap and shout!
Birthday song,
Sing along!
Oh!

Continued

CHORUS

Will you read your birthday card?
Yes, I'll read my birthday card!
Birthday card,
Laugh so hard!
Birthday cake,
Here, please take!
Candles out,
Clap and shout!
Birthday song,
Sing along!
Oh!

CHORUS

Will you have some party fun?
Yes, I'll have some party fun!
Party fun,
Everyone!
Birthday card,
Laugh so hard!
Birthday cake,
Here, please take!
Candles out,
Clap and shout!
Birthday song,
Sing along!
Oh!

CHORUS

The 100th Day of School

(sung to "The Ants Go Marching One by One")

We've all been counting one by one,
Hurrah, hurrah!
We've all been counting, oh, what fun,
Hurrah, hurrah!
We've all been counting one by one,
And now 100 days are done!
Hooray!
Today's the 100th day of school!

We started counting up to 10,
Hurrah, hurrah!
To 20, 30, 40, then,
Hurrah, hurrah!
To 50, 60, 70, then
To 80, 90, and now is when—
Hooray!
Today's the 100th day of school!

We started with a number low,
Hurrah, hurrah!
And one by one, we made it grow,
Hurrah, hurrah!
We started with a number low,
And now it's grown to 1-0-0,
Hooray!
Today's the 100th day of school!

What's the Season?

(sung to "Old MacDonald Had a Farm")

After summer, it turns cool.

What's the season?

Fall!

Now we all return to school.

What's the season?

Fall!

CHORUS:

Oh, the red leaves fall,

And the yellow leaves fall!

Orange leaves, gold leaves,

Brown leaves, all the leaves!

After summer, it turns cool.

What's the season?

Fall!

There's a tool we need to take.

What's the season?

Fall!

Gather leaves up with a rake.

What's the season?

Fall!

CHORUS

Playing football's fun to do.

What's the season?

Fall!

Picking apples is fun, too.

What's the season?

Fall!

CHORUS

Halloween is on its way.

What's the season?

Fall!

And soon we'll have Thanksgiving Day.

What's the season?

Fall!

CHORUS

Fire Prevention Week

(sung to "The Farmer in the Dell")

Fire Prevention Week,
Fire Prevention Week,
The week of October 9
Is Fire Prevention Week.

Never start a fire.
Never start a fire.
Remember Fire Prevention Week.
Never start a fire.

Don't play with matches.
Don't play with matches.
Remember Fire Prevention Week.
Don't play with matches.

Report a fire you see.
Report a fire you see.
Remember Fire Prevention Week.
Report a fire you see.

Fire Prevention Week,
Fire Prevention Week,
The week of October 9
Is Fire Prevention Week.

Happy Halloween!

(sung to "Row, Row, Row your Boat")

Carve, carve carefully,
Carve a pumpkin clean.
On October 31,
Happy Halloween!

Carve, carve carefully,
Carve a pumpkin face.
Give it a nose and eyes and teeth.
Then set it in its place!

Trick, trick, trick-or-treat,
Everywhere you go.
Wear a costume, oh what fun!
Surprise the friends you know.

Trick, trick, trick-or-treat,
Laugh along the way.
By the end of Halloween,
Your bag is full, hooray!

National Children's Book Week

(sung to "Skip to My Lou")

CHORUS:

Read, read, read a book.

Read, read, read a book.

Read, read, read a book.

It's National Children's Book Week!

The third week of November is here.

That's a special time of year,

Celebrating something dear—

National Children's Book Week!

CHORUS

Find a book and start to read.

One good book is all you need.

You will have such fun indeed!

National Children's Book Week!

CHORUS

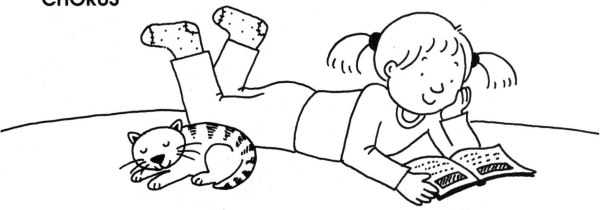

Choose a book of any kind.
What adventures you will find!
See the action in your mind.
National Children's Book Week!

CHORUS

Many places you will go,
Characters you'll get to know.
It's better than a TV show!
National Children's Book Week!

CHORUS

Share a book with your best friend.
Read the book from start to end.
Be the characters, just pretend!
National Children's Book Week!

CHORUS

We Celebrate Thanksgiving!

(sung to "Ten Little Indians")

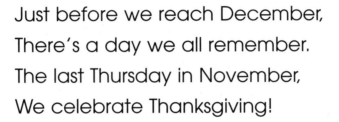

Just before we reach December,
There's a day we all remember.
The last Thursday in November,
We celebrate Thanksgiving!

We give thanks for what we eat.
We give thanks for warmth and heat.
We give thanks for friends we meet.
Let's celebrate Thanksgiving!

We give thanks for clothes we wear.
We give thanks for things to share.
We give thanks to show we care.
Let's celebrate Thanksgiving!

We give thanks for rain and sun.
We give thanks for having fun.
We give thanks for everyone.
Let's celebrate Thanksgiving!

We give thanks for work and play.
We give thanks for each new day.
We give thanks in every way.
Let's celebrate Thanksgiving!

Winter Holidays of Light

(sung to "Do You Know the Muffin Man?")

CHORUS:
Do you know the holidays,
The holidays, the holidays?
Do you know the holidays
We celebrate with light?

Christmas lights are on the tree,
Nice and bright for all to see.
Christmas with the family,
We celebrate with light.

CHORUS

Hanukkah has lots of lights.
See the menorah glow eight nights.
Hanukkah, with candles bright,
We celebrate with light.

CHORUS

Kwanzaa has its lights ablaze.
Light the kinara on seven days.
Kwanzaa brings such joy in ways
We celebrate with light.

CHORUS

Las Posadas, what a treat,
Candles carried in the street,
Smile at everyone you meet,
We celebrate with light.

CHORUS

St. Lucia Day is filled with cheer.
People hold their candles near.
The longest evening of the year,
We celebrate with light.

CHORUS

New Year's Day!

(sung to "Three Blind Mice")

New Year's Eve, New Year's Eve,
December 31, December 31,
I'm so excited, that is clear!
A brand-new year is almost here!
I'll stay up late to give a cheer
On New Year's Eve!

New Year's Day, New Year's Day,
January 1, January 1,
I love it when the year is new.
So many things I plan to do.
I'm so excited, yes, it's true,
On New Year's Day!

New Year's Day, New Year's Day,
A brand-new year, a brand-new year,
I'll fill my calendar with a plan
For the new year that just began.
There's not a time more hopeful than
New Year's Day!

Martin Luther King, Jr. Day

(sung to "Hush, Little Baby, Don't Say a Word")

In January, the third Monday
Is Martin Luther King, Jr. Day.

A day to remember Dr. King,
A day to recall his important dream.

A dream of peace and harmony,
A dream of true equality.

A dream of standing proud and tall,
A dream of freedom and justice for all.

A dream of love and friendship, too.
A dream for me and a dream for you.

In January, respects we pay
On Martin Luther King, Jr. Day.

Today on Groundhog Day

(sung to "Where, Oh Where, Has My Little Dog Gone?")

CHORUS:
Where, oh, where will the groundhog go?
Will it leave? Will it stay?
The answer's found when it pops from the ground
Today on Groundhog Day!

Oh, February the second is here,
And that's exciting to me!
We watch the way that the groundhog behaves
To learn what the weather may be.

CHORUS

If the groundhog looks out of his hole
And sees his shadow appear,
He climbs back down to his home in the ground,
Six more weeks of winter, oh dear!

CHORUS

But if the groundhog looks out of his hole
And sees no shadow—hooray!
He climbs right out and then scurries about,
For spring is well on its way!

CHORUS

Will You Be My Valentine?

(sung to "Baa, Baa, Black Sheep")

February 14th, hip hooray!
Time to celebrate Valentine's Day!
Sending valentines is fun,
Sharing joy with everyone.
I'll be yours if you'll be mine.
Will you be my Valentine?

February 14th, hip hooray!
Let's make a valentine today.
Bright red paper cut like a heart,
Decorated with pretty art.
Make a colorful design.
Will you be my Valentine?

February 14th, hip hooray!
Time to celebrate Valentine's Day!
Valentines are nice to send.
Share your love with each good friend.
I'll be yours if you'll be mine.
Will you be my Valentine?

A Snow Day!

(sung to "It's Raining, It's Pouring")

It's snowing, it's falling,
A snow day is calling.
School is closed 'cause on the roads
The cars and trucks are stalling!

A snow day, a snow day,
A watch-the-snowflakes-blow day,
Let's get dressed and ride a sled,
A sledding-we-will-go day!

A snow day we're taking.
A snowman we are making.
Later on we'll have cocoa
And hot cakes that are baking.

A snow day, a snow day . . . *(fade voice)*

In the Spring!

(sung to "If You're Happy and You Know It")

You can see the flowers bloom in the spring!
You can see the flowers bloom in the spring!
You can see the flowers bloom,
And the bees around you zoom.
You can see the flowers bloom in the spring!

It is fun to fly a kite in the spring!
It is fun to fly a kite in the spring!
It is fun to fly a kite,
When the breezy wind is right.
It is fun to fly a kite in the spring!

You can hear the birdies tweet in the spring!
You can hear the birdies tweet in the spring!
You can hear the birdies tweet,
And the grass smells, oh, so sweet.
You can hear the birdies tweet in the spring!

You can watch a rainy shower in the spring!
You can watch a rainy shower in the spring!
You can watch a rainy shower.
Raindrops fall on every flower.
You can watch a rainy shower in the spring!

Hooray for Earth Day!

(sung to "Down by the Station")

Hooray for Earth Day,
April 22,
A day for us
To celebrate Earth.
Hooray for Earth Day,
April 22.
Let's praise the world
For all it is worth!

Earth has air
We all need for breathing.
Earth has trees
That give us fruit to eat.
Earth has grass
That cattle use for grazing.
Earth has sunlight
To give us light and heat.

Earth has oceans
That give us water.
Water for people
And water for fish.
Earth has mountains
That add a lot of beauty.
Earth has everything
We could ever wish!

Hooray for Earth Day,
April 22,
A day for us
To recognize its worth.
Hooray for Earth Day,
April 22.
Let's count the ways
That we can help Earth.

Plant lots of trees and
Lots of pretty flowers.
Place all your garbage
In a bag or can.
Don't waste water.
Don't waste energy.
Learn to recycle.
That's a helpful plan!

Happy May Day

(sung to "Daisy, Daisy")

May Day, May Day,

Here on the first of May,

Celebrating spring in a special way!

Let's go to the park for hours,

Enjoy the pretty flowers.

They smell so sweet,

And look so neat.

In the wind, how they dance and sway!

May Day, May Day,

Marking the joys of spring.

In the sunshine, oh, how we'll dance and sing!

We'll play in the nice, warm weather.

We'll have such fun together!

The first of May,

A special day,

What happy times it will bring!

It's Flag Day!

(sung to "Camptown Races")

June 14, a special date—
Flag Day, Flag Day!
It's a time to celebrate,
Celebrate our flag!

Wave it proudly in the air.
Flag Day, Flag Day!
Show how much you truly care.
Celebrate our flag!

CHORUS:
Cheer the Stars and Stripes!
Cheer the U.S.A.!
Cheer the flag, a symbol of
Our country, hip hooray!

Take the flag and wave it high.
Flag Day, Flag Day!
Join parades as they go by.
Celebrate our flag!

Hold the flag for all to see.
Flag Day, Flag Day!
Tell of all its history.
Celebrate our flag!

CHORUS

In the Summer

(sung to "Are You Sleeping?")

In the summer, in the summer,
Days are hot, days are hot.
I enjoy a nice drink.
I enjoy a cold drink.
Drink a lot, drink a lot!

In the summer, in the summer,
I keep cool, I keep cool.
I like to go swimming.
I like to go swimming
In the pool, in the pool!

In the summer, in the summer,
I feel free, I feel free.
Time for recreation,
Time for a vacation,
Happily, happily.

In the summer, in the summer,
I have learned, I have learned,
At the beach or ocean,
Wear your suntan lotion.
Don't get burned, don't get burned!

We Celebrate Our Freedom!

(sung to "Bingo")

July 4th is a special day
When we declared our freedom!

CHORUS:
Independence Day,
Independence Day,
Independence Day,
We celebrate our freedom!

Back in 1776,
The bells rang out for freedom!

CHORUS

The U.S.A. was born that day
When we declared our freedom!

CHORUS

Wave the flag to celebrate.
We celebrate our freedom!

CHORUS

Watch parades and fireworks, too.
We celebrate our freedom!

CHORUS

Feathers, Scales, and Fur

(sung to "Do You Know the Muffin Man?")

CHORUS:

Do you know the animals,
The animals, the animals?
Do you know the animals
With feathers, scales, and fur?

Birds have feathers so they'll fly.
They help the birds soar through the sky.
They keep them warm and safe and dry.
Yes, feathers are for birds!

CHORUS

Fish have scales, oh yes, they do.
Snakes and lizards have them, too.
The hard, flat scales protect, it's true.
These animals have scales!

CHORUS

Most mammals have fur, you see,
A dog, a rabbit, and monkey,
A squirrel and chipmunk in the tree.
Most mammals have warm fur!

CHORUS

Migration! Migration!

(sung to "There Were Ten in the Bed")

In wintertime, some animals roam
To find themselves a warmer home.
Migration! Migration!

Some birds fly south, that's their thing.
They don't return until the spring.
Migration! Migration!

In winter, some butterflies swarm.
They all head south, where it is warm.
Migration! Migration!

In winter, some whales find they need
Warmer waters in which to breed.
Migration! Migration!

They all migrate when temperatures drop.
They find a new home, and there they stop!
Migration! Migration!

In spring, the birds and butterflies roam,
And like the whales, they come back home.
Migration! Migration!

The Life of a Frog

(sung to "Down by the Station")

Life for a frog
Begins in early April.
Males call to females,
Looking for a mate.
In ponds large and small,
The frogs do their breeding.
The females lay eggs.
Then they wait.

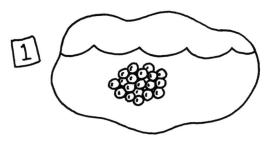

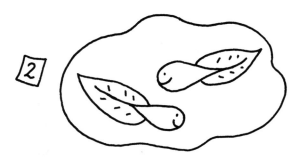

The eggs hatch tadpoles,
And each grows so quickly,
Reaching its adult size
By early July.
The tadpole starts changing
And grows into a frog now.
Hop! Hop! Gulp! Gulp!
Eating a fly!

In summer and autumn,
The frog is very busy,
Gulping down the insects,
Hunting 'til late.
But when winter comes
The frog hops to the forest.
It is time to
Hibernate!

Under the forest floor,
The frog is still and frozen.
It sits just like an ice cube
Hard and cold.
But when spring returns,
The frog hops to the pond again.
Happy birthday,
One year old!

Spiderwebs

(sung to "The Itsy Bitsy Spider")

A busy, busy spider
Is weaving with its thread.
Watch how the spider
Weaves a spiderweb.
The thread is silk
That the spider makes,
And the web has a pattern
That rarely ever breaks!

Some spiders shape
Their webs like a dome.
Some spiders weave
A triangle home.
Some spiders make
Their webs so nice and round.
So many different kinds
Of webs can be found!

Homes All Around

(sung to "Home on the Range")

Most birds like to rest

In a grass-and-twig nest,

While bees make their home in a hive.

And you can find bears

Well protected in lairs.

Yes, a home helps each creature survive.

CHORUS:

Homes, homes all around,

Many animal homes can be found,

Way up in a tree,

On the floor of the sea,

In the grass, or deep under the ground.

Continued

The home for a frog
May be inside a log,
While a crab makes its home in a shell.
And you'll find a mole
Underground in a hole,
Where a burrow protects it quite well.

CHORUS

You'll find many snakes
In their homes around lakes,
While beavers build lodges of wood.
And monkeys are pleased
To live high in the trees,
While bats find a cave to be good.

CHORUS

Animals Live in the Forest

(sung to "I've Been Working on the Railroad")

Animals live in the forest,
Roaming in the woods.
Animals live in the forest,
In tree-lined neighborhoods.
See the very busy squirrel
In a hollow tree trunk it's found.
See the very lazy turtle
In a log on the ground.

Animals live in the forest.
There's a big brown bear.
Animals live in the forest,
In a cave that's called a lair.
Look! A hopping rabbit hurries
To its burrow fast as can be.
Hear! A woodpecker is pecking
For insects in a tree!

Animals live in the forest,
Elk and moose and deer.
Animals live in the forest,
Oh, so many creatures here!
Owls are sitting on a tree branch,
Calling, "Hoo, hoo, hoo!"
Animals live in the forest.
"Wood" you like a home there, too?

Home in the Water

(sung to "Pop! Goes the Weasel")

By a riverbank, you will find
A friendly, furry otter.
A snake creeps into a river to sleep,
Home in the water.

A frog is fond of life in a pond.
A whale is a globe-trotter.
It swims around in the ocean blue,
Home in the water.

A duck makes its home by a lake,
And swims when days are hotter.
A salmon's dream is life in a stream,
Home in the water.

Snapping turtles chomp in a swamp,
They go there when it's hotter.
Crocodiles swim 'round there, too,
Home in the water.

Animals in the Desert

(sung to "My Bonnie Lies Over the Ocean")

Some animals live in the desert,
Where living can get very hot.
Lizards and rats you will find there,
And foxes you also can spot.

CHORUS:

Desert, desert,
Where animals live in their homes, their homes.
Desert, desert,
Where animals live in their homes.

Scorpions crawl by the bushes,
And spiders stay under the rocks.
Cottontails hide in their burrows,
Deep down where no enemy knocks.

CHORUS

Deep in the Rain Forest

(sung to "Rock-a-Bye Baby in the Treetop")

Deep in the rain forest, in the treetops,
Animals live where rain rarely stops.
Shelters are formed by leaves in the trees,
Making three layers called canopies.

In the top layer, toucans are found.
Monkeys and bats stay far off the ground.
Hummingbirds sip the nectar from flowers,
While upside-down sloths just hang out for hours!

In the middle layer, there's much more to see.
Lemurs and squirrels fly from tree to tree.
Marmosets leap up high without fail.
Opossums and porcupines hang by their tail.

In the bottom layer—the rain forest floor,
Hogs give a snort, while leopards all roar.
Anteaters dine on ants that they see,
While big pythons slither 'round roots of a tree.

Deep in the rain forest, in the treetops,
Animals live where rain rarely stops.
Shelters are formed by leaves in the trees,
Making three layers called canopies.

The Food Chain

(sung to "The Farmer in the Dell")

A green plant grows.
A green plant grows.
Let's explain the food chain.
A green plant grows.

A bug eats the plant.
A bug eats the plant.
Let's explain the food chain.
A bug eats the plant.

A mouse eats the bug.
A mouse eats the bug.
Let's explain the food chain.
A mouse eats the bug.

An owl eats the mouse.
An owl eats the mouse.
Let's explain the food chain.
An owl eats the mouse.

Continued

The owl lives out its life.
The owl lives out its life.
Let's explain the food chain.
The owl lives out its life.

Its body feeds a plant.
Its body feeds a plant.
Let's explain the food chain.
Its body feeds a plant.

A green plant grows.
A green plant grows.
Let's explain the food chain.
A green plant grows.

The Parts of a Plant

(sung to "The Wheels on the Bus")

The roots on a plant grow underground,
Underground, underground.
The roots on a plant grow underground.
Roots are part of a plant.

The stems on a plant hold up the leaves,
Up the leaves, up the leaves.
The stems on a plant hold up the leaves.
Stems are part of a plant.

The leaves on a plant are making food,
Making food, making food.
The leaves on a plant are making food.
Leaves are part of a plant.

The flowers on a plant are growing seeds,
Growing seeds, growing seeds.
The flowers on a plant are growing seeds.
Seeds are part of a plant.

An Apple Tree Year

(sung to "Here We Go 'Round the Mulberry Bush")

CHORUS:

Here we go 'round, go 'round the year,

'Round the year, 'round the year.

Here we go 'round, go 'round the year,

To watch an apple tree growing!

In spring, the apple blossoms grow.

Pink-white flowers start to show.

Bees visit them to and fro.

An apple tree in the springtime!

CHORUS

In summer, there's a change to see.

Blossoms fall right off the tree.

Leaves are growing full and free.

An apple tree in the summer!

CHORUS

In fall, the tree has something new—
Ripe, round apples, quite a few!
Picking them is what we'll do.
An apple tree in the autumn.

CHORUS

In wintertime, the tree is bare.
A chilly wind is in the air.
No leaves or apples anywhere,
An apple tree in the winter.

CHORUS

Seed to Pumpkin

(sung to "Hush, Little Baby, Don't Say a Word")

Hey, pretty pumpkin, how did you grow?
Tell us the story, we'd like to know.

I grew from a tiny pumpkin seed,
Planted in some good soil, yes, indeed!

The seed was planted at the end of May.
It received sun and water every day.

Leaves sprouted out and grew and grew.
Soon yellow flowers came out, too.

The flowers died and left pumpkin fruit.
I was one of those pumpkins, oh, so cute!

I grew every day as months went by,
I became a big pumpkin. My, oh my!

And that's the story of how I did grow,
From seed to pumpkin, now you know!

Rain and Snow

(sung to "Three Blind Mice")

Rain and snow, rain and snow,

My, what a show! My, what a show!

At times, the rain showers really pour.

At times, the snow piles up at my door.

I'd like to know all the causes for

The rain and snow!

What brings rain? What brings rain?

Clouds in the sky, clouds in the sky.

The clouds are where all the rain is stored.

And when the clouds just can't hold anymore,

The raindrops fall and it starts to pour.

That brings rain!

What brings snow? What brings snow?

Clouds in the sky, clouds in the sky.

Small crystals form when the air starts to freeze.

They fall from the sky and are blown by the breeze.

The snowflakes fall on the houses and trees.

That brings snow!

A Constellation

(sung to "Twinkle, Twinkle, Little Star")

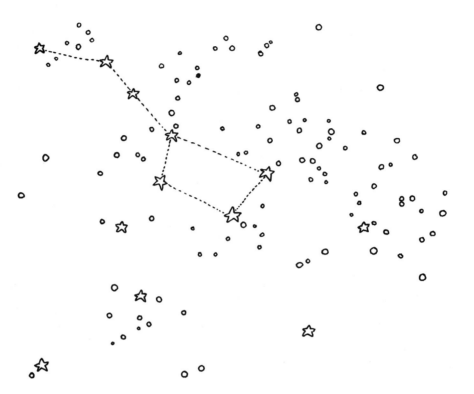

Twinkle, twinkle, group of stars,
A constellation is what you are.
Form a shape up in the sky.
Shine so bright as you pass by.
Twinkle, twinkle, group of stars.
A constellation is what you are.

Twinkle, twinkle, stars of fame,
Each constellation has a name.
The Big Dipper is nice to view.
The Little Dipper is famous, too.
Twinkle, twinkle, group of stars,
A constellation is what you are.

I Have Got a Shadow

(sung to "I'm a Little Teapot")

I have got a shadow
On the ground.
All through the day
It hangs around.
Its shape is always changing
With the sun.
Watching it
Can sure be fun!

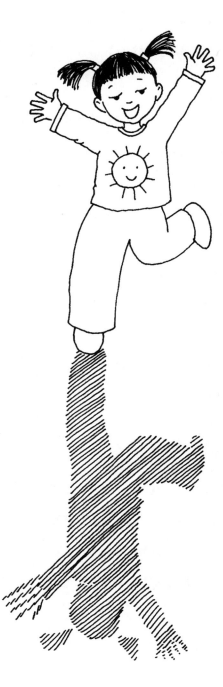

When I walk to school,
What do I see?
I see my shadow
Follow me.
Everywhere I go,
My shadow's there.
See?
It tracks me everywhere!

I have got a shadow
On the ground.
All through the day
It hangs around.
But when there's no light,
It is not here.
At night,
My shadow disappears!

Build Your Muscles

(sung to "Good Night, Ladies")

CHORUS:

Buiid your muscles,

Build your muscles,

Build your muscles,

To give you muscle power!

Merrily we bend and stretch,

Bend and stretch, bend and stretch.

Merrily we bend and stretch

To build our muscle power!

CHORUS

Merrily we run and jog,

Run and jog, run and jog.

Merrily we run and jog

To build our muscle power!

CHORUS

Merrily we do sit-ups,

Do sit-ups, do sit-ups.

Merrily we do sit-ups

To build our muscle power!

CHORUS

Merrily we skip a rope,
Skip a rope, skip a rope.
Merrily we skip a rope
To build our muscle power!

CHORUS

Merrily we do push-ups,
Do push-ups, do push-ups.
Merrily we do push-ups
To build our muscle power!

CHORUS

Merrily we ride a bike,
Ride a bike, ride a bike.
Merrily we ride a bike
To build our muscle power!

CHORUS

The Key to Energy

(sung to "Are You Sleeping?")

Are you eating, are you eating
Healthy foods, healthy foods?
Practice good nutrition.
Practice good nutrition.
That's the key
To energy!

Are you eating, are you eating
Wholesome grains, wholesome grains?
Bread and rice and bagels,
Cereal and noodles,
They're the key
To energy!

Are you eating, are you eating
Veggies and fruit, veggies and fruit?
Carrots and potatoes,
Apples and tomatoes,
They're the key
To energy!

Are you eating, are you eating
Healthy meats, healthy meats?
Chicken, beef, and fish
And turkey are delish!
They're the key
To energy!

Are you eating, are you eating
Dairy foods, dairy foods?
Yogurt, milk, and cheeses,
Dairy food that pleases.
They're the key
To energy!

Use Your Five Senses

(sung to "If You're Happy and You Know It")

When you look and when you see, use your eyes.
When you look and when you see, use your eyes.
When you look and when you see
All the things there are to see,
When you look and when you see, use your eyes!

When you listen and you hear, use your ears.
When you listen and you hear, use your ears.
When you listen and you hear
All the things there are to hear,
When you listen and you hear, use your ears!

When you touch and when you feel, use your hands.
When you touch and when you feel, use your hands.
When you touch and when you feel
All the things there are to feel,
When you touch and when you feel, use your hands!

When you lick and when you taste, use your tongue.
When you lick and when you taste, use your tongue.
When you lick and when you taste
All the things there are to taste,
When you lick and when you taste, use your tongue!

When you sniff and when you smell, use your nose.
When you sniff and when you smell, use your nose.
When you sniff and when you smell
All the things there are to smell,
When you sniff and when you smell, use your nose!

Do Your Toes Stay Clean?

(sung to "Do Your Ears Hang Low?")

Do your toes stay clean?
Do you soap them in between?
Do you scrub your ears
So no dirt appears?
Do you wash each hand
After playing in the sand?
That is good hygiene!

As you know, hygiene
Means keeping very clean,
Getting germs off quick
So you don't get sick.
Taking baths or showers
So you'll be clean for hours.
That is good hygiene!

Do you wash your hair,
Shampooing everywhere?
Do you scrub your feet
So they smell so sweet?
Do you brush your teeth
To clean off the food you eat?
That is good hygiene!

Sunny Day Safety

(sung to "Sing a Song of Sixpence")

Sing a song of safety
On bright and sunny days.
Keep yourself protected
In important ways.
Always wear a sun hat
When the day is hot.
Being in the sun is fun,
But getting burned is not!

Sing a song of safety
Under sunny skies.
Wear a pair of sunglasses
To protect your eyes.
Put on lots of sunscreen
When the day is hot.
Being in the sun is fun,
But getting burned is not!

Riding Bikes Is Lots of Fun!

(sung to "London Bridge Is Falling Down")

Riding bikes is lots of fun,
Lots of fun, lots of fun.
Riding bikes is lots of fun,
When you're careful.

Snap a helmet on your head,
On your head, on your head.
Snap a helmet on your head
To protect you.

Ride around the neighborhood,
Neighborhood, neighborhood.
Ride around the neighborhood,
Far from traffic.

Keep away from cars and trucks,
Cars and trucks, cars and trucks.
Keep away from cars and trucks
When you're riding.

At the corner, you must stop,
You must stop, you must stop.
At the corner, you must stop.
Watch for traffic.

Slow down if a person's near,
Person's near, person's near.
Slow down if a person's near.
Keep your distance.

Riding bikes is lots of fun,
Lots of fun, lots of fun,
Riding bikes is lots of fun,
When you're careful!

Walking Is Such Fun!

(sung to "Row, Row, Row, Your Boat")

Walk, walk, walk around
In your neighborhood.
Walking can be lots of fun,
Walking's very good!

Walk, walk, walk along,
Watch your step and feet.
Walk upon the sidewalk, friend,
Never in the street.

Look, look, look ahead.
See the traffic light.
Wait until it tells you "Walk."
Then look left and right.

Cross, cross, cross the street.
Walk, but do not run.
When you follow safety rules,
Walking is such fun!